MEDITATIONS FOR PASCHA

Meditations for Pascha

REFLECTIONS ON THE PENTECOSTARION

Vassilios Papavassiliou

ANCIENT FAITH PUBLISHING
CHESTERTON, INDIANA

Scripture quotations are taken from the New King James
Version, © 1979, 1980, 1982 by Thomas Nelson, Inc. Used
by permission.

Published by:
    Ancient Faith Publishing
    P.O. Box 748
    Chesterton, IN 46304
Printed in the United States of America

ISBN: 978-1-936270-25-5

Cover calligraphy by Jan Powell
Interior design by Katherine Hyde

20 19 18   13 12 11 10 9 8 7 6 5 4 3 2

Contents

Introduction

Bless God in the congregations,
The Lord, from the fountain of Israel.
(Entrance hymn of the Pascha
season; Ps. 67[68]:26)

THE LIFE-GIVING SPRING, THE POOL OF Bethesda, the well of the Samaritan woman, the pool of Siloam—one image permeates the season of the *Pentecostarion*: water. The *Pentecostarion* is the main hymnbook of the Pascha season, or Eastertide (the forty days between Pascha and the Ascension), and its hymns are sung in church until the Sunday after Pentecost (All Saints' Day).

In the ancient Church, Christians were baptized at Pascha, when they celebrated with the rest of the Church their incorporation into the redeemed Body of Christ and their participation in the life of the Resurrection and of the Holy Spirit. Later the Feast of Pentecost also became a day on which Christians received baptism. Hence the central theme of water, reminding us of the waters of baptism, through which we become "partakers of the divine nature" (2 Pet. 1:4) and of the heavenly Kingdom.

The *Pentecostarion* takes its name from *Pentecost,* which is the Greek term for the Feast of Weeks—an ancient Jewish holiday still celebrated in Judaism as *Shavuot.* The Feast of Weeks commemorates the anniversary of the day God gave the Law to the people of Israel on Sinai. Just as the date of *Shavuot* is linked to that of Passover, the date of Pentecost is linked to that of the Christian Passover (Pascha). It was on the day of

Pentecost, fifty days after our Lord's Resurrection (*Pentecost* means "fiftieth day"), that the Holy Spirit descended upon the Apostles and upon all flesh (Acts 2:1–38; Joel 2:28–29), and it is this event that Orthodox Christians celebrate every year on the Feast of Pentecost.

Despite holding such a central position in the Church's worship for eight weeks of the year, no hymnbook is so overlooked as the *Pentecostarion*. Throughout Lent and Holy Week, we have been building up to the joyful celebration of our Lord's Resurrection. The Pascha season (which we will henceforth refer to simply as "Pascha") is therefore considered a time to feast and rejoice: the Wednesday and Friday fasts are abolished in the week after Pascha, or throughout the whole season according to another ancient Orthodox tradition. It certainly is a time for rejoicing, but this should not lead us to forget that it is also a preparation for another great feast: Pentecost.

The season of the *Pentecostarion* can be divided into two halves, with the Feast of Mid-Pentecost acting as a watershed between the celebration of Pascha and the preparation for Pentecost. From Pascha to Mid-Pentecost there is a greater emphasis on the Resurrection, while from Mid-Pentecost the emphasis shifts to the coming feast and the waters of baptism. Pascha is therefore both backward-looking and forward-looking: we celebrate and rejoice in our Lord's Resurrection, and we prepare for the great feast of the Holy Spirit descending upon us, filling and fulfilling the Church of Christ. The risen Christ will return to His Father in heaven (the Ascension), and the Holy Spirit will come down to us on earth (Pentecost).

This descent of the Holy Spirit and His indwelling within us is one of the principal themes of Christian Orthodox baptism. Every year, the Church reminds us of our own baptism (however long ago it may have occurred) and the incredible calling to be vessels of the Holy Spirit. The Church therefore lays before us an important and humbling question: Am I living up to my sacred calling to be a disciple of Christ and a member of His Church? It is upon this question that this little book invites us to reflect.

A Guide to the Season of the Pentecostarion

Pascha and Renewal Week/Bright Week
The Pascha season begins. Sunday of Pascha through Thomas Sunday

The Life-Giving Source
Friday of Renewal Week

Thomas Sunday
First Sunday after Pascha

The Myrrh-bearing Women
Second Sunday after Pascha

The Paralytic
Third Sunday after Pascha

Mid-Pentecost
Fourth Wednesday after Pascha

The Samaritan Woman
Fourth Sunday after Pascha

The Blind Man
Fifth Sunday after Pascha

Leave-taking of Pascha
Sixth Wednesday after Pascha. The Pascha season ends.

The Ascension
Sixth Thursday after Pascha

Sunday of the Fathers of the First Ecumenical Council
Sixth Sunday after Pascha

All Souls' Saturday
Sixth Saturday after Pascha

Pentecost Sunday
Seventh Sunday after Pascha

Trinity Week
Week following Pentecost Sunday

All Saints' Day
Sunday after Pentecost

⇥ 1 ⇤

Renewal and Illumination

RENEWAL WEEK/BRIGHT WEEK

Come, let us drink a new drink, not one wondrously brought forth from a barren rock,[1] but the Source of immortality, which springs forth from the tomb of Christ, in whom we are established. (Third ode of the Canon of Pascha, Sunday of Pascha)

THE WEEK FOLLOWING PASCHA IS KNOWN as Renewal Week, since all things have been made new by the Lord's Resurrection. "Therefore, if anyone *is* in Christ, *he is* a new creation; old things

---

1   Exodus 17:1–7

have passed away; behold, all things have become new" (2 Cor. 5:17). It is also called Bright Week, since the Resurrection has enlightened all things:

> Now all things have been filled with light, both heaven and earth and those beneath the earth; so let all creation sing of Christ's rising, by which it is established. (Canon of Pascha, troparion of the third ode)

The whole of Renewal Week, or Bright Week, is a celebration of Pascha. Yet even now, the theme of Pentecost is already present, particularly in the image of the "spring" or "fountain" of life—reminiscent of our Lord's words to the Samaritan woman, which is the theme of the fifth Sunday of Pascha:

> "Whoever drinks of the water that I shall give him will never thirst. But the water that I shall give him will become in him a fountain of water springing up into everlasting life." (John 4:14)

This image becomes apparent on the Friday of Renewal Week, when "we celebrate the conse-cration of the temple of our most-holy Lady, the Mother of God of the Life-giving Spring" (Synax-arion of the Friday of Renewal Week):

> *O Virgin Mother of God, for me you now pour forth grace from the Fount, thus granting me eloquence to praise your Spring, which pours forth life and grace for the faithful; for from you flowed forth the Incarnate Word. (First ode of the Canon to the Mother of God, Friday of Renewal Week)*

> *I know you to be a radiant and holy temple of the Master of all, O Maiden, and a Spring whence sprang forth Christ, the Water of immortality, wherefrom we are given to drink. (Third ode of the Canon to the Mother of God, Friday of Renewal Week)*

The Life-giving Spring is an epithet of the Holy Mother of God that originated with her reve-lation of a sacred spring in Constantinople to a soldier named Leo Marcellus, who later became Byzantine Emperor Leo I (457–474). Leo built the historic Church of St. Mary of the Spring over this site, which witnessed numerous miraculous healings over the centuries. The feast reminds us of our due veneration of the Mother of God as the source of that wellspring of life which is Jesus Christ, who ascended to the Father that He might send down the Holy Spirit to us (John 14:15; 15:26).

These three themes of the week after Pascha—water, light, and renewal—bring to mind the words of the ablution said at our baptism:

> *You have been justified. You have been enlightened. You have been sanctified. You have been cleansed in the name of our Lord Jesus Christ and by the Spirit of God. You have been baptized. You have been illumined. You have been anointed with myrrh. You have been hallowed. You have been washed clean. In the name of the*

*Father and of the Son and of the Holy Spirit.
Amen.*

In remembering these words, we are reminded
that our lives should reflect the calling of our
baptism to "become worthy of the incorruptible
Kingdom . . . to be a child of light and heir of eternal blessings . . . a partaker in the death and resurrection of Christ our God," and to "preserve the
garment of Baptism and the pledge of the Holy
Spirit unblemished and undefiled on the dread
Day of Christ our God" (Litany of Holy Baptism).
Have we continued to walk in the light?

> If we say that we have fellowship with Him, and
> walk in darkness, we lie and do not practice the
> truth. But if we walk in the light as He is in the
> light, we have fellowship with one another, and
> the blood of Jesus Christ His Son cleanses us
> from all sin. (1 John 1:6–7)

⇥ 2 ⇤

The Body of Christ

THOMAS WEEK

Today is the spring of souls, for Christ, shining forth from the tomb like the sun, has dispelled the foggy winter of sin. Let us sing to Him, for He has been glorified. (Canon of Thomas Sunday, troparion of the first ode)

THE SUNDAY AFTER PASCHA—THOMAS Sunday—is known as *Antipascha*, meaning "Instead of Pascha." Those who were unable to attend the Agape Vespers (Vespers of Love) on the evening of Pascha Sunday, when we hear the

⇥ 21 ⇤

Gospel reading regarding Christ's Resurrection and His appearance to the Apostles (John 20:19–25), are able to hear that Good News on Thomas Sunday. The central theme of the Gospel reading for the day (John 20:19–31) is Thomas's conversion from unbelief to belief in the Resurrection, in Christ as Lord and God:

> Then, the same day at evening, being the first *day* of the week, when the doors were shut where the disciples were assembled, for fear of the Jews, Jesus came and stood in the midst, and said to them, "Peace *be* with you." When He had said this, He showed them *His* hands and His side. Then the disciples were glad when they saw the Lord. So Jesus said to them again, "Peace to you! As the Father has sent Me, I also send you." And when He had said this, He breathed on *them,* and said to them, "Receive the Holy Spirit. If you forgive the sins of any, they are forgiven them; if you retain the *sins* of any, they are retained."
>
> Now Thomas, called the Twin, one of the

twelve, was not with them when Jesus came. The other disciples therefore said to him, "We have seen the Lord." So he said to them, "Unless I see in His hands the print of the nails, and put my finger into the print of the nails, and put my hand into His side, I will not believe."

And after eight days His disciples were again inside, and Thomas with them. Jesus came, the doors being shut, and stood in the midst, and said, "Peace to you!" Then He said to Thomas, "Reach your finger here, and look at My hands; and reach your hand *here,* and put *it* into My side. Do not be unbelieving, but believing." And Thomas answered and said to Him, "My Lord and my God!" (John 20:19–28)

While the Resurrection is the central theme of our hymns and readings, the image of water is still present, particularly in the theme of our Lord's side, reminding us of how "one of the soldiers pierced His side with a spear, and immediately blood and water came out" (John 19:34):

The Cross was fixed in Calvary and blossomed forth immortality for us from the ever-flowing fountain that is the side of the Savior. (First hymn of the aposticha, Vespers of Thomas Wednesday)

The Church Fathers see in the water and blood a reference to the two great sacraments through which we become one with Christ: Baptism and the Eucharist. As St. John Chrysostom writes:

I said that there was a symbol of baptism and the mysteries[2] in that blood and water. It is from both of these that the Church is sprung *through the bath of regeneration and renewal by the Holy Spirit,* through baptism and the mysteries. But the symbols of baptism and the mysteries come from the side of Christ. It is from His side, therefore, that Christ formed His church, just as He formed Eve from the side of Adam.

. . . Just as at that time God took the rib of Adam and formed a woman, so Christ gave us blood and water from His side and formed the

---

2   The Eucharist

Church. Just as then He took the rib from Adam when he was in a deep sleep, so now He gave us blood and water after His death, first the water and then the blood. But what was then a deep slumber is now a death, so that you may know that this death is henceforth sleep.[3]

The relationship between Christ and His Church is as intimate as that between Adam and Eve, between husband and wife. As the Church of Christ, we are called to become "one flesh" with our Lord. How can we sinners possibly be made worthy of such a union with the holy and divine unless we are first purified of our sins and passions?

> Let us exhibit zeal to sanctify our profane hands by cutting off the passions. Thus shall we be able to touch the Master's pure and holy side. (First hymn of the Praises, Matins of Thomas Wednesday)

---

3   *Ancient Christian Writers, St. John Chrysostom: Baptismal Instructions* (New York/Mahwah: Paulist Press, 1963), p. 62

Consecrate, O my soul, the senses of your body to godly contemplation; for so does Christ the Lord desire you to be renewed. (Second hymn of the Praises, Matins of Thomas Wednesday)

Let dejection born of the passions and tempestuous thoughts be banished. Thus shall the springtime of faith sprout up and blossom forth. (Thomas Thursday, first hymn of the Praises)

Faith is the main theme of Thomas Sunday, and faith is not determined by words alone, but also by deeds. True belief is not a mere nod of approval to a set of ideas, but conviction acted upon, which shapes our lives and informs our choices. As St. James writes:

What *does it* profit, my brethren, if someone says he has faith but does not have works? Can faith save him? If a brother or sister is naked and destitute of daily food, and one of you says to them, "Depart in peace, be warmed and filled," but you do not give them the things which are needed for the body, what *does it* profit? Thus also faith by itself, if it does not have works, is dead. But someone will say, "You have faith, and I have works." Show me your faith without your works, and I will show you my faith by my works. (James 2:14–18)

If we continue to wallow in the mire of sin, if we continue to behave as though we were not temples of the Holy Spirit, but as if our bodies belonged to us rather than to Him, we will not be fit to receive the Holy Spirit anew and to be the dwelling place of God. This is why the Lord says:

"You shall be holy to Me, for I the LORD *am* holy, and have separated you from the peoples, that you should be Mine." (Lev. 20:26)

This notion of belonging to God is powerfully conveyed in the act of Chrismation, when we are anointed with myrrh (the holy Chrism) at baptism, and we hear the words, "The seal of the gift of the Holy Spirit." This seal can be compared to a mark of ownership, signifying that we are the property of God:

> Do you not know that your bodies are members of Christ? . . . [H]e who is joined to the Lord is one spirit *with Him* . . . [D]o you not know that your body is the temple of the Holy Spirit *who is* in you, whom you have from God, and you are not your own? For you were bought at a price; therefore glorify God in your body and in your spirit, which are God's. (1 Cor. 6:15, 17, 19–20)

If our bodies are temples of the Holy Spirit, then they are God's possessions and not ours. Therefore, spiritual life, or rather, "Spirit-bearing" life, means a sacrifice of the self. As we hear in the service of Baptism, "Reckon yourselves to be dead indeed to sin, but alive to God in Christ Jesus our Lord" (Rom. 6:11).

❧ 3 ❧

Tears and Myrrh

WEEK OF THE
MYRRH-BEARING WOMEN

This feast of the women who brought myrrh and of the august, noble Joseph has now appeared unto us as another Paradise bringing a fountain of life. It wells up for all the world with waters of grace, and it pours forth in strength the streams of the Resurrection. Wherefore the faithful keep feast and cry out: Glory to Him who bestows grace and Resurrection upon all the world. (Monday of the Myrrh-bearing Women, Vespers, third hymn of the stichera)

On the third Sunday of Pascha, we commemorate the Myrrh-bearing Women, who went to the tomb of Christ to anoint His body, only to find the tomb empty and an angel declaring that He had risen:

> Now when the Sabbath was past, Mary Magdalene, Mary *the mother* of James, and Salome bought spices, that they might come and anoint Him. Very early in the morning, on the first *day* of the week, they came to the tomb when the sun had risen. And they said among themselves, "Who will roll away the stone from the door of the tomb for us?" But when they looked up, they saw that the stone had been rolled away—for it was very large.
>
> And entering the tomb, they saw a young man clothed in a long white robe sitting on the right side; and they were alarmed. But he said to them, "Do not be alarmed. You seek Jesus of Nazareth, who was crucified. He is risen! He is not here. See the place where they laid Him. But go, tell His disciples—and Peter—that He is

going before you into Galilee; there you will see Him, as He said to you." (Mark 16:1–7)

Two images that are a recurring theme in our hymns remind us of baptism: tears and myrrh.

Why do you mingle tears with myrrh, O women disciples? The stone has been rolled away, the tomb is empty. Behold, decay has been trodden under by Life, the seals bear witness, the guards of the disobedient are fast asleep. Mortal nature is saved by the flesh of God, and Hades laments. Hasten with joy and tell the Apostles: Christ, the First-born of the dead, has slain death and goes before you into Galilee. (Vespers for the Sunday of the Myrrh-bearing Women, second hymn of the stichera of the Myrrh-bearers)

The women sprinkled myrrh with tears upon Your tomb; and their mouth was filled with joy, saying: The Lord has risen! (Matins for the Sunday of the Myrrh-bearing Women, fifth hymn of the Praises)

Grieving, the myrrh-bearing women who fol-
lowed Christ cried out.... But while they were
weeping, an angel spoke to them of godly joy,
saying: Christ the Lord has risen! Make haste,
proclaim to all people His divine resurrection
from the tomb! (Matins for the Wednesday of
the Myrrh-bearing Women, fourth hymn of the
Praises)

While myrrh reminds us of the holy chrism (in Greek, *myron*) with which we are anointed in baptism, signifying the descent of the Holy Spirit upon us, tears of righteous sorrow and repentance are described in Orthodox literature as a renewal of baptism. As St. John of the Ladder writes:

The tears that come after baptism are greater than baptism itself, though it may seem rash to say so. Baptism washes off those evils that were previously within us, whereas the sins commit-ted after baptism are washed away by tears. The baptism received by us as children we have all defiled, but we cleanse it anew with our tears.[4]

4   *John Climacus: The Ladder of Divine Ascent,* The Classics of

The Myrrh-bearing Women went to the tomb of Christ in tears of sorrow, only to have them transformed into tears of joy and gladness. So too does Christ transform our tears of repentance into tears of gratitude for His love and forgiveness. However much we may have defiled our baptism, however short we have fallen of our calling to be children of light and vessels of the Holy Spirit, there is still hope. For our tears wash away our sins as do the waters of baptism.

It may seem a contradiction, but the tears of repentance are a wellspring of joy. The *Pentecostarion* thus continues in positive terms the same "bright sadness" that characterizes the *Lenten Triodion*. For every time we repent, we are washed clean, receiving anew a pure and resurrected life. Therefore, let us pray:

> *Gather my scattered mind, O Lord, and purify my hardened heart. Grant me repentance, even*

Western Spirituality (New York: Paulist Press, 1982), p. 137

as You did to Peter; and sighs of the heart, as You did to the publican; and tears, as You did to the harlot, that with a mighty voice I may cry to You: Save me, O God, for You alone are compassionate and the Lover of mankind. (Tuesday of the Paralytic, Matins, second hymn of the stichera of the Praises)

⇾ 4 ⇽

Spiritual Paralysis

WEEK OF THE PARALYTIC

Of old an angel came down to the Sheep's Pool and healed one person every year; but now Christ cleanses endless multitudes by divine Baptism. (Canon of the Sunday of the Paralytic, fourth troparion of the first ode)

ON THE SUNDAY OF THE PARALYTIC, WE hear the following Gospel passage:

There was a feast of the Jews, and Jesus went up to Jerusalem. Now there is in Jerusalem by the Sheep *Gate* a pool, which is called in Hebrew,

Bethesda, having five porches. In these lay a great multitude of sick people, blind, lame, paralyzed, waiting for the moving of the water. For an angel went down at a certain time into the pool and stirred up the water; then whoever stepped in first, after the stirring of the water, was made well of whatever disease he had.

Now a certain man was there who had an infirmity thirty-eight years. When Jesus saw him lying there, and knew that he already had been *in that condition* a long time, He said to him, "Do you want to be made well?" The sick man answered Him, "Sir, I have no man to put me into the pool when the water is stirred up; but while I am coming, another steps down before me." Jesus said to him, "Rise, take up your bed and walk." And immediately the man was made well, took up his bed, and walked. (John 5:1–8)

What a horribly familiar scene! Countless sick and disabled people flock to the pool, seeking healing. It reminds me of many a visit of a holy relic or miracle-working icon to a church, or of a famous site of pilgrimage. Thousands may come together for what appears to be a religious motive, but each person comes for himself, seeking not a more intimate experience of God but a cure for whatever physical illness ails him. And the moment one has an opportunity to be healed, he rushes forward without a care for anyone else. For thirty-eight years, this paralytic found no one, not a single "religious" person to help him; not one who even considered loving his neighbor as himself! All these sick people were ailing with a terrible spiritual illness: selfishness.

The story of the paralytic is above all a cautionary tale of spiritual paralysis. Our souls are paralyzed by self-love, unable to lift a finger to help another at our own expense. Certainly most of us show concern for others, and many of us may do "a good deed for the day," but when it is a matter of "him or me," more often than not, the choice is "me." This is the sickness of which all of us are in need of healing, a healing for which we must all cry out to Christ in repentance.

"Do you want to be made well?" the Church asks us every Pascha. And let us not say, as did the paralytic, "I have no one." The paralytic thought he had no one to help him, no one who loved him, but he had the Lord Himself, as do all of us. He loves us with a pure, selfless love. Even if all others in the Church care only for themselves and their own, we have not been abandoned. For God is the guardian of orphans and widows, of the meek and defenseless, of the oppressed and forlorn (Ex. 22:22–23, Ps. 11[12]:5).

The Sheep's Pool was the site of a miracle of healing that took place once a year. But now comes One greater than the angel who descended into the pool to cure physical sickness: here is One who offers healing of the soul to all people, in all places, at all times. He offers us baptism in "the Holy Spirit and fire" (Matt. 3:11), a purifying fire that burns up all our sins and illumines the heart; a baptism of "water and the Spirit" (John 3:5) that washes away our iniquities and cleanses the soul.

Do we want to be made well? Do we wish to be cured of incurable selfishness? Do we desire to love our neighbor as ourselves? Do we long to become worthy of Christ's baptism? If so, let us bring forth the fruits of repentance, let us renew our baptism with tears, and let us heed the hymn:

O barren and unfruitful soul, bring forth good works, that bearing comely fruits, you may cry: My heart is established; there is none holy and there is none righteous but You, O Lord. (Canon of the Sunday of the Paralytic, third ode, hirmos of the Paralytic)

⇌ 5 ⇌

Wash and Be Clean

MID-PENTECOST

Now has come the middle of the days which begin with Christ's saving Resurrection and which are sealed by that divine day of Pentecost. Enlightened by both feasts, and joining both, it is made radiant and resplendent, manifesting and revealing the presence of the great glory of the Ascension of our Master, Christ. (Vespers for the Wednesday of Mid-Pentecost, first hymn of the stichera)

DURING THE VESPERS ON THE EVE OF THE Wednesday of Mid-Pentecost, we hear in the reading from Isaiah:

Everyone who thirsts,
Come to the waters . . .
Seek the Lord while He may be found,
Call upon Him while He is near.
Let the wicked forsake his way,
And the unrighteous man his thoughts;
Let him return to the Lord,
And He will have mercy on him;
And to our God,
For He will abundantly pardon.
(Is. 55:1, 6–7)

Our failure to live up to the calling of baptism—to a life of purity, righteousness, and illumination—is made very explicit at Mid-Pentecost. Yet the recognition of this failure is full of hope in the mercy of God "who desires all men to be saved and to come to the knowledge of the truth" (1 Tim. 2:4). With the remembrance of our shortcomings comes the first step to the solution: turn to God in confession and repentance.

Wash yourselves, make yourselves clean;
Put away the evil of your doings from before My
　　eyes.
Cease to do evil,
Learn to do good;
Seek justice,
Rebuke the oppressor;
Defend the fatherless,
Plead for the widow.
"Come now, and let us reason together,"
Says the Lord,
"Though your sins are like scarlet,
They shall be as white as snow;
Though they are red like crimson,
They shall be as wool." (Is. 1:16–18)

The feast of Mid-Pentecost, and indeed the whole season of the *Pentecostarion*, is a period of joy and brightness, and yet the *Pentecostarion* is not without hymns of compunction. Just as the period of Great Lent is not void of the light of the Resurrection, so too the period of Pascha is not void of the theme of repentance. The light of Pascha and

Pentecost compels us to recognize the darkness within us and to seek purity and renewal that we may be able to fully share in the joy and holiness of the Spirit:

> As we come together on the mid-feast between Your Resurrection and the divine descent of Your Holy Spirit, O Christ, we praise the mysteries of Your wonders. Wherefore, on this day send down upon us Your great mercy. (Vespers for the Wednesday of Mid-Pentecost, doxastikon of the stichera)

Mid-Pentecost strengthens our preparation for Pentecost—a preparation which requires a renewal of faith and an intensified effort to ascend the heights of righteousness and purity to which we were called when we became members of Christ's Body. The joy of Pascha lies in a vigorous response to the Resurrection and the presence of the Holy Spirit within us and around us. The more sensitive to His presence we become, the more aware we become of our own sins. And our response to this sinfulness is not a paralyzing despair, but a renewed hope and desire to be filled with the Holy Spirit:

> *Since we have learned from Christ a new and unprecedented way of life, let us all be especially diligent to preserve it until the end, that we may enjoy the presence of the Holy Spirit. (Canon of Matins for the Wednesday of Mid-Pentecost, first troparion of the ninth ode)*

～ 6 ～

Spirit and Truth

WEEK OF THE SAMARITAN WOMAN

The abundant outpouring of the Divine Spirit upon all is now at hand, as the Scripture says. This is proclaimed by the midpoint of the blessed period after the death, burial, and resurrection of Christ our God, when He gave His disciples His unfailing and true promise, which clearly revealed and made manifest the coming of the Comforter. (Vespers of the Sunday of the Samaritan Woman, third hymn of the stichera of Mid-Pentecost)

"GIVE ME A DRINK." SO BEGINS ONE OF THE most profound dialogues in the Gospels—that between Christ and a woman of Samaria:

So He came to a city of Samaria which is called Sychar, near the plot of ground that Jacob gave to his son Joseph. Now Jacob's well was there. Jesus therefore, being wearied from *His* journey, sat thus by the well. It was about the sixth hour. A woman of Samaria came to draw water. Jesus said to her, "Give Me a drink." For His disciples had gone away into the city to buy food. Then the woman of Samaria said to Him, "How is it that You, being a Jew, ask a drink from me, a Samaritan woman?" For Jews have no dealings with Samaritans. Jesus answered and said to her, "If you knew the gift of God, and who it is who says to you, 'Give Me a drink,' you would have asked Him, and He would have given you living water." The woman said to Him, "Sir, You have nothing to draw with, and the well is deep. Where then do You get that living water? Are You greater than our father Jacob, who gave us the well, and drank from it himself, as well as his sons and his livestock?" Jesus answered and said to her, "Whoever drinks of this water will thirst again, but whoever drinks of the water that I shall give him will never thirst. But the water that I shall give him will become in him a fountain of water springing up into everlasting life." . . .

The woman said to Him, "Sir, I perceive that You are a prophet. Our fathers worshiped on this mountain, and you *Jews* say that in Jerusalem is the place where one ought to worship." Jesus said to her, "Woman, believe Me, the hour is coming when you will neither on this mountain, nor in Jerusalem, worship the Father. You worship what you do not know; we know what we worship, for salvation is of the Jews. But the hour is coming, and now is, when the true worshipers will worship the Father in spirit and truth; for the Father is seeking such to worship Him. God *is* Spirit, and those who worship Him must worship in spirit and truth." The woman said to Him, "I know that Messiah is coming" (who is called Christ). "When He comes, He will tell us

all things." Jesus said to her, "I who speak to you
am *He.*" (John 4:5–13, 19–26)

The Samaritans were heretics who accepted
only the first five books of the Old Testament.
They also believed Mount Gerazim—one of the
highest peaks in the West Bank in the vicinity
of the city Nablus (Shechem in the Bible)—and
not Jerusalem to be the one true sanctuary and
holy place of God. We see in the Gospel passage
a reference to an all-too-familiar religious quar-
rel: God is here, not there; we, not they, are the
chosen people of God; the Lord is on our side,
not theirs.

And now our Lord overturns this religious
narrow-mindedness and arrogance with one
simple phrase: "In Spirit and truth." Through the
Holy Spirit, all who are baptized will become the
dwelling place of God:

"The kingdom of God does not come with
observation; nor will they say, 'See here!' or 'See

there!' For indeed, the kingdom of God is within you." (Luke 17:20–21)

Through the Holy Spirit, we are all made temples of God. This gift of becoming vessels of the Holy Spirit is freely offered to all, rich and poor, Jew and Gentile, saint and sinner. The Church invites us to draw from the well of repentance, to wash ourselves clean in the tears of contrition, and to be made new, that we may be fit for the Holy Spirit to abide within us:

Wash me with my tears, O Savior, for I am defiled by many sins. Wherefore, I fall down before You. I have sinned; have mercy on me, O God. (Matins of the Tuesday of the Samaritan Woman, second hymn of the Praises)

When the compassionate Lord came to the well, the Samaritan woman entreated Him, saying: Grant me the water of faith, and I shall receive the waters of the font of baptism for gladness and redemption. O Giver of life, Lord, glory to You. (Vespers of the Sunday of the Samaritan

Woman, second hymn of the stichera of the Samaritan woman)

The references to the water of life in the Gospel reading for the Sunday of the Samaritan woman are vividly expressed in St. John the Evangelist's description of the establishment of God's heavenly Kingdom on earth:

> "I will give of the fountain of the water of life freely to him who thirsts. He who overcomes shall inherit all things, and I will be his God and he shall be My son. . . ." And he showed me a pure river of water of life, clear as crystal, proceeding from the throne of God and of the Lamb. . . . And the Spirit and the bride say, "Come!" And let him who hears say, "Come!" And let him who thirsts come. Whoever desires, let him take the water of life freely. (Rev. 21:6–7; 22:1, 17)

This places Pentecost in the context of the "last days" (in Greek, the *eschata*), that is to say, in the context of the Second Coming and the fulfillment of God's Kingdom. The life of the world to come has already broken through, and in the Holy Spirit we already sense that "the tabernacle of God *is* with men, and He will dwell with them, and they shall be His people. God Himself will be with them *and be* their God.... They shall see His face, and His name *shall be* on their foreheads" (Rev. 21:3; 22:4).

Through baptism we are made members of Christ's Body, heirs of His Kingdom and inheritors of His eternal blessings. Though we have all made ourselves unworthy of these, He came into the world to pour upon us His great mercy and to wash us in the baptism of His Blood and in the waters of humility. Having returned to the heavenly Father, from whom He is eternally begotten and from whom the Holy Spirit forever proceeds forth, He poured the Holy Spirit upon us that we may have God living within us, transforming and renewing us from within. The Holy Spirit never abandons us, and no matter how often we reject Him and cast Him from us, He returns to all who repent, longing to fill us with His abundant love and the joy of salvation:

> On this mid-feast does Christ our God, the mighty river of divine glory, bestow the streams of His great compassion upon all, and He cries out: You that are thirsty, come and draw for yourselves. He pours out forgiveness upon the world, since He is in truth a gulf of mercy and a wellspring of compassion. He purges our sins and expunges our maladies. He saves those who keep the memorial of His Resurrection and protects those who honor and celebrate with longing His Ascension in glory. And He grants to our souls His peace and great mercy. (Vespers of the Monday of the Samaritan Woman, second hymn of the stichera)

❧ 7 ❧

See the Light

WEEK OF THE BLIND MAN

O Christ our God, spiritual Sun of Righteousness, who by Your pure touch bestowed two kinds of illumination upon him who from his mother's womb was deprived of sight, enlighten the eyes of our souls also, and prove us to be children of the day, that we may cry to You with faith: Great and unsearchable is Your compassion toward us, O Lover of mankind; glory to You. (Vespers for the Sunday of the Blind Man, doxastikon of the stichera)

On the Sunday of the Blind Man, we hear the following Gospel passage:

Now as *Jesus* passed by, He saw a man who was blind from birth. And His disciples asked Him, saying, "Rabbi, who sinned, this man or his parents, that he was born blind?" Jesus answered, "Neither this man nor his parents sinned, but that the works of God should be revealed in him. I must work the works of Him who sent Me while it is day; *the* night is coming when no one can work. As long as I am in the world, I am the light of the world." When He had said these things, He spat on the ground and made clay with the saliva; and He anointed the eyes of the blind man with the clay. And He said to him, "Go, wash in the pool of Siloam" (which is translated, Sent). So he went and washed, and came back seeing....

Now it was a Sabbath when Jesus made the clay and opened his eyes.... Therefore some of the Pharisees said, "This Man is not from God, because He does not keep the Sabbath." Others said, "How can a man who is a sinner do such signs?" And there was a division among them. They said to the blind man again, "What do you say about Him because He opened your eyes?" He said, "He is a prophet." . . . Then they said to him again, "What did He do to you? How did He open your eyes?" He answered them, "I told you already, and you did not listen. Why do you want to hear *it* again? Do you also want to become His disciples?" Then they reviled him and said, "You are His disciple, but we are Moses' disciples. We know that God spoke to Moses; *as for* this *fellow,* we do not know where He is from." The man answered and said to them, "Why, this is a marvelous thing, that you do not know where He is from; yet He has opened my eyes! Now we know that God does not hear sinners; but if anyone is a worshiper of God and does His will, He hears him. Since the world began it has been unheard of that anyone opened the eyes of one who was born blind. If this Man were not from God, He could do nothing." They answered and said to him, "You were completely born in sins, and are you teaching us?" And they cast him out.

Jesus heard that they had cast him out; and when He had found him, He said to him, "Do you believe in the Son of God?" He answered and said, "Who is He, Lord, that I may believe in Him?" And Jesus said to him, "You have both seen Him and it is He who is talking with you." Then he said, "Lord, I believe!" And he worshiped Him. (John 9:1–7, 16–17, 26–38)

While the image of water is still present with the pool of Siloam, the *Pentecostarion* now places greater emphasis on another theme of baptism and of Pentecost: illumination.

I worship the Father as Light, I glorify the Son as Light, and I praise the Upright Spirit as Light: one undivided Light, perceived in three persons, the God and King of all creation. (Matins of the Sunday of the Blind Man, Canon of the Blind Man, doxastikon of the ninth ode)

The story of the blind man is not only a miracle of healing, but above all a tale of enlightenment. We may gain a clearer understanding of the Gospel reading if we read on from where the passage breaks off:

> And Jesus said, "For judgment I have come into this world, that those who do not see may see, and that those who see may be made blind." Then *some* of the Pharisees who were with Him heard these words, and said to Him, "Are we blind also?" Jesus said to them, "If you were blind, you would have no sin; but now you say, 'We see.' Therefore your sin remains." (John 9:39–41)

The Pharisees, being learned men who knew the Law and the Prophets, were without excuse— they should have known better—but the blind man lived in the darkness of ignorance. We who have been enlightened through baptism and who know the Scriptures cannot plead ignorance. Like the scribes and Pharisees, we are without excuse. If we are blind to the Light of love and truth, it is because we prefer the darkness:

> "And this is the condemnation, that the light has come into the world, and men loved darkness rather than light, because their deeds were evil." (John 3:19)

When the blind man washes his eyes in the Pool of Siloam, he receives his physical sight, but spiritually he is still blind, still ignorant of the truth. This is clear from two erroneous statements the man makes before Christ is revealed to him. When the Pharisees ask him what he makes of the man who gave him his sight, he replies, "He is a prophet." So thought many others, even though they had seen Him with their own eyes. The truth, however, is what St. Peter said when Christ asked the Apostles, "Who do you say that I am?" Peter replied, "You are the Christ, the Son of the Living God" (Matt. 16:15–16).

Later, the blind man says, "We know that God does not hear sinners." If God does not hear sinners, then what hope is there for any of us?

What would have become of all the sinners who repented and became saints? What would have become of the sinful publican who begged God to have mercy on him? (Luke 18:10–14). If God did not hear sinners, the publican would not have gone home justified as Christ tells us he did. The once-blind man still does not know the merciful God.

When our Lord sees the man after he has received his sight, He asks him, "Do you believe in the Son of God?" "Who is He, Lord," he inquires, "that I may believe in Him?" And in our Lord's reply, we see the meaning of the miracle. Like a loving father revealing his identity to the son who never knew him, He responds: "You have both seen Him and it is He who is talking with you." Does the man doubt? Not for a second, but exclaims, "Lord, I believe!" Having received his spiritual sight, he recognizes Christ as God, falls at His feet, and worships Him. And at last, he can see the Light; at last, he can see the Truth.

It is this invitation to see and walk in the light that is extended to us in the hymns for the week of the blind man. Let us not walk in the darkness of sin and ignorance, but in the light of the Holy Trinity, which is the light of truth and righteousness:

> Enlighten my spiritual eyes, which are bereft of sight, O Lord, because of the gloomy darkness of sin. And since You are compassionate, instill in me humility. Cleanse me by the tears of repentance and change my heart. (Matins of the Sunday of the Blind Man, exapostilarion)

> Since the spiritual eyes of my soul are blind and sightless, I come to You, O Christ, as did the man born blind. And in repentance I cry to You: You are the most radiant Light of those in darkness. (Matins of the Sunday of the Blind Man, kontakion)

⇥ 8 ⇤

Divine Ascent

LEAVE-TAKING OF PASCHA AND ASCENSION THURSDAY

The Lord has been taken up into heaven, that He may send the Comforter to the world. The heavens have prepared His throne, the clouds His ascent. Angels marvel to see a human high above them. The Father receives Him whom He holds eternally in His bosom. The Holy Spirit orders all His angels, "Lift up your gates, you rulers." All you nations, clap your hands: for Christ has gone up where He was before. (Vespers for Ascension Thursday, first hymn of the stichera)

*P*ASCHA CONCLUDES WITH THE LEAVE-taking of Pascha, when we again celebrate the Paschal liturgy, and for the last time we greet one another with the words, "Christ is risen!" — "Truly the Lord is risen!"

The following day, forty days after Pascha, we celebrate our Lord's Ascension into heaven. Some have come to think of this day as a sorrowful one, because the Lord is physically no longer present with us on earth but returns to the Father. But it is by no means a day of sorrow, for in ascending to the heavenly Father, our Lord took with Him our human nature, which He assumed for our salvation. Because He shares in our humanity, we share in His divinity; because He became our brother, we are children of His Father:

> "I am ascending to My Father and your Father, and *to* My God and your God." (John 20:17)

"I go to prepare a place for you. And if I go and prepare a place for you, I will come again and receive you to Myself; that where I am, *there* you may be also." (John 14:2–3)

Because Christ took flesh, died, and rose in the body and raised it up to heaven, we are able to follow Him to God the Father:

> *When You came down from heaven to things on earth and as God raised up with You Adam's nature, which lay below in the prison of Hades, You brought it to heaven by Your Ascension, O Christ, and made it sit with You on Your Father's throne, for You are merciful and love mankind. (Matins of the Ascension, kathisma)*

As St. Paul writes:

> Now this, "He ascended"—what does it mean but that He also first descended into the lower parts of the earth? He who descended is also the One who ascended far above all the heavens, that He might fill all things. (Eph. 4:9–10)

Far from being a day of sorrow, the Ascension is a feast of joy and eager anticipation. We cannot think of the Ascension without remembering that Christ is returning to the Father to pour the Holy Spirit upon us:

> *You were taken up in glory, Christ our God, giving joy to Your Disciples by the promise of the Holy Spirit, when through the blessing they had been assured that You are the Son of God, the Redeemer of the world. (Apolytikion of the Ascension)*

> *In ascending to heaven, O Lord, from where You also descended, do not leave us orphans; may Your Spirit come, bringing peace to the world; show to the sons of men Your powerful deeds, O Lord, for You love mankind. (Vespers for Ascension Thursday, first hymn of the aposticha)*

As our Lord said:

> "It is to your advantage that I go away; for if I do not go away, the Helper will not come to you; but if I depart, I will send Him to you." (John 16:7)

With Pentecost approaching, again we are reminded of baptism through the image of water in our church services. In the third Old Testament reading for the Vespers of the Ascension, we hear:

> Behold, the day of the LORD is coming,
> And in that day His feet will stand on the
>   Mount of Olives,
> Which faces Jerusalem on the east.
> And in that day it shall be
> *That* living waters shall flow from Jerusalem,
> Half of them toward the eastern sea
> And half of them toward the western sea;
> In both summer and winter it shall occur.
> And the LORD shall be King over all the earth.
> In that day it shall be—
> "The LORD *is* one,"
> And His name one. (Zech. 14:1, 4, 8–9)

While the Ascension invites us to strengthen our preparation for Pentecost, at the same time it reminds us strongly of our Lord's Second Coming:

Your angels, O Lord, said to Your Apostles: Men of Galilee, why do you stand looking up to heaven? This is Christ our God, who is taken up from you into heaven; He will come again in the same way that you have seen Him going to heaven;[5] serve Him in holiness and righteousness. (Vespers for Ascension Thursday, third hymn of the aposticha)

This double preparation characterizes the Feast of the Ascension: We prepare for the coming of the Holy Spirit while remembering also the Second Coming of Christ. Again, Pentecost and baptism are placed within the context of the last things. For through the Holy Spirit, we are given a foretaste of the world to come. Therefore, the Church calls us always to be ready for the coming of the Lord:

Abandoning on earth the things of the earth, leaving to the dust the things of the dust, let us now come to our senses and lift up our eyes

5   Acts 1:9–11

and minds. O mortals, let our sight and all our senses fly to the gates of heaven. Let us imagine we are standing on the Mount of Olives, turning our gaze on the Redeemer as He rides upon a cloud. For from where the Lord has hastened back to heaven, there too the Beneficent One has distributed His gifts to His Apostles, cherishing them as a father and confirming them, guiding them as sons and saying, "I am not parting from you. I am with you, and there is no one against you." (*Matins of the Ascension, ikos*)

✦ 9 ✦

The Doctrine of the Holy Trinity

SUNDAY OF THE HOLY FATHERS OF NICEA

Let us heed the Church of God as she cries out with the lofty proclamation: Whoever is thirsty, let him come to me and drink; the bowl that I carry is the bowl of truth; the drink in it I have mixed with the word of truth, pouring in not the water of contradiction but that of confession; the new Israel, as he drinks from it, sees God, who declares: Lo and behold, it is I; I have not changed; I am God, the first and the last, and there is none beside me. Those who partake from here shall be filled and praise the great mystery of true religion. (Matins of the Ascension, ikos)

ON THE SUNDAY AFTER THE ASCENSION, we commemorate the Holy Fathers of the First Ecumenical Council, which took place in Nicea in 325. It was at this Holy Council that the Creed of the Church began to be formed. The Council condemned the widespread heresy of Arianism that was plaguing the Church, a heresy which declared that the Son of God is a created being, and not, as the Orthodox believe, co-eternal with the Father. And so we sing on this day:

Let us praise today the mystical trumpets of the Spirit, the God-bearing Fathers, who sang a harmonious melody of theology in the midst of the Church: one Trinity, an unchanging Essence and Godhead; the overthrowers of Arius, the champions of the Orthodox, who ever intercede with the Lord that He have mercy on our souls. (Vespers of the Ascension, doxastikon of the stichera)

The reason we celebrate this event on the Sunday between Ascension Thursday and Pentecost Sunday is given to us in the Synaxarion for the Holy Fathers of Nicea:

> We celebrate the present feast for the following reason. Since our Lord Jesus Christ, who had put on our flesh, had ineffably accomplished the whole dispensation and was reinstated on his Father's throne, the saints—wishing to show that the Son of God had truly become man and that, as perfect man, God had ascended and had sat down at the right of the Majesty on high— this synod of the holy Fathers proclaimed and confessed Him to be of one essence and identical in honor with the Father; for this reason they appointed this present Feast after the glorious Ascension, as it were putting forward the assembly of so many Fathers proclaiming this, that the one who was taken up in the flesh was God and in the flesh perfect man.
>
> This Council took place under Constantine the Great in the twentieth year of his reign.... Then too began the business of Arius. He came

originally from Libya. After coming to Alexandria, he was ordained deacon by Peter the Martyr Bishop of Alexandria. Then he began to utter blasphemies against the Son of God, declaring that He had come into being from non-existence and was far from the divine dignity and that it was only by analogy that he was called Wisdom and Word of God.... Arius was the first to utter that Christ was of a mutable nature and that the Lord had assumed flesh without mind or soul....

Because the Church was greatly troubled and there appeared no cure for the love of strife concerning doctrine, Constantine the Great gathered the Fathers from all over the inhabited world by public transport to the city of Nicea... the Word of God was proclaimed to be consubstantial, identical in honor, and without beginning with the Father. They also issued the holy Symbol of the faith, taking it as far as "and in the Holy Spirit"; for the rest was completed by the second Council. (Matins of the Ascension, Synaxarion)

The doctrine of the Holy Trinity is summed up in the Symbol of Faith, which we recite at every Divine Liturgy. It is a baptismal creed that is said (supposedly by heart) before we are received into the Church. When we are baptized, we are bound to the doctrines of the Church, to belief in the Holy Trinity as one God known in three Persons: Father, Son, and Holy Spirit. In baptism the Holy Spirit Himself comes to dwell within us and enlighten us, and the doctrine of the Holy Trinity reminds us that this means we will become vessels of God Himself:

> *The Holy Spirit always was, and is, and will be, neither beginning nor coming to an end, but always ranked and numbered with the Father and the Son; life and giver of life; light and bestower of light; goodness itself and source of goodness; through whom the Father is known and the Son glorified and by all is known, one power, one order, one worship of the Holy*

Trinity. (*Matins of Pentecost Sunday, second hymn of the Praises*)

Baptism is not to be taken lightly: through it we are made vessels of the Holy Spirit and witnesses of divine truth. If our faith is not that of the Church, we are not fit for baptism. Let us therefore not be idle when it comes to matters of theology, but let us take them seriously as part and parcel of Christian spirituality.

Unfortunately, the connection between theology and spirituality is frequently ignored. On the one hand, some hold the view that knowledge of God means theology in the academic sense of the word. That is to say, if one reads enough and agrees to all the Church's doctrines, knows the Ecumenical Councils, and (perhaps most importantly of all) knows the difference between Orthodoxy and other forms of Christianity, he knows God. It is almost a snobbish and elitist understanding of divine knowledge. Just as some of us clergy don't know the difference between liturgy and liturgics, many Orthodox don't know the difference between knowledge of God and knowledge about God.

On the other hand, some hold the view that knowledge of God means mysticism. That is to say, we consider all theological study and discussion to be scholastic, intellectual, even sinful. All we need do is listen to our spiritual father, say our prayers, go to church, and read about lives of saints, even if we have no intention of imitating them. And if any intelligent unbeliever challenges us about our religion, we dismiss such arguments with appeals to faith over reason, emotion over intellect, and obedience over common sense.

The Fathers of the First Ecumenical Council did not subscribe to either of these views. They fought tooth and nail for precise theological definitions, which to most Christians today seem petty. Is Christ *homoousios* (of one essence) with the Father, or *homoiousios* (of a similar essence) to the Father? Is Christ created or uncreated? That was the division which was plaguing the Church in the fourth century and which the First Ecumenical Council was called to put an end to. But Christians have continued to argue, sometimes with violent consequences, throughout the ages.

So fed up have Christians become with religious arguments that many have simply given up caring about such theology. But the disagreements go on. Still many Christians speak of Christ as nothing more than a mortal man, rather than eternal God. Were the Holy Fathers of Nicea not rejoicing in heaven, I would be tempted to say they are turning in their graves!

But for all their unyielding concern for correct doctrine, they were not academic snobs. They did not believe that understanding theological definitions meant knowledge of God, as important as correct theology is. The Holy Fathers were people of love and prayer, and this love and prayer did not involve abandoning dogma or intellect. Orthodox mysticism is not a vague, personal experience of God based on each individual's feelings, ideas, and experiences; and to be spiritual does not mean to be an intellectual slacker, as though God had no interest in our minds and didn't ask us to give those to Him along with the rest of us. Mysticism without theological truth is subjective and delusional, and theology without mysticism is nothing but an academic hobby.

What the Fathers of the First Ecumenical Council exemplify is the fullness of the human being—mind, body, and spirit—completely occupied with God. They lived and breathed theology, real theology. They knew Scripture back-to-front, they prayed ceaselessly, they stripped themselves of wealth to help the poor. Yet not once did they consider that what one believes is not important. Rather, the same passion we see in their theological writings and their desire to put an end to the heresies of the day we see also in their daily lives, in their repentance and pursuit of holiness. They are what it means to be completely consumed by the love of God. This, for me, is the great example we have before us in the Fathers of the First Ecumenical Council.

We go on making our excuses: "Surely God wouldn't mind if . . ." "Surely God doesn't care that . . ." "Surely we can't live like the saints of the past." Oh, but we can, and we must. Not in the sense, as some Orthodox seem to think, that we must constantly be on the attack or on the defensive against heresies, but in the sense that we must acquire the same passion for God they possessed, a passion that made them give their all—their time and energy, their minds and bodies, their wealth and possessions, even their very lives—to God.

The Holy Fathers of Nicea have shown us what it means to "know You, the only true God, and Jesus Christ whom You have sent" (John 17:3). May we learn to follow their example.

~ 10 ~

The God of the Living

ALL SOULS' SATURDAY AND KNEELING VESPERS OF PENTECOST SUNDAY

Accept, O Master, our supplications and entreaties, and give rest to the fathers and mothers, brothers and sisters, and children of each, and to every other kinsman and relative, and to all the souls who have gone to their rest before us in the hope of resurrection to eternal life. Establish their spirits and their names in the book of life and in the bosoms of Abraham, Isaac, and Jacob, in the land of the living, the Kingdom of heaven, the Paradise of pleasure. Through Your radiant angels bring them into Your holy mansions. With them raise our bodies also on the day which You have appointed in accordance with Your holy and unfailing promise. For there is no death for Your servants, Lord, when we go out from the body and come to You, O God, but a translation from sorrow to things better and more desirable, and rest and joy. (Third prayer of Kneeling Vespers, Pentecost Sunday)

ON THE FRIDAY BEFORE PENTECOST, THE celebration of the Feast of the Ascension comes to an end, and on All Souls' Saturday (the day before Pentecost) we remember and pray for all Orthodox departed. Our sharing in the community of baptized Orthodox Christians that is the Church cannot be taken from us, even by death. For as St. Paul writes:

For I am persuaded that neither death nor life, nor angels nor principalities nor powers, nor things present nor things to come, nor height nor depth, nor any other created thing, shall be able to separate us from the love of God which is in Christ Jesus our Lord. (Rom. 8:38–39)

For this reason we pray for those who have departed this life in hope of Resurrection. This practice goes back even to the Old Testament:

But under the tunics of each of the dead, they uncovered sacred tokens of the Jamnian idols, which the Jews are forbidden by law to wear. ... They turned to supplication and prayed that the sin they had committed might be blotted out. The noble Judas ... then took up an offering from his soldiers amounting to two thousand silver drachmas, and sent it to Jerusalem to present as a sin offering. In doing so he acted properly and with honor, taking note of the resurrection of those fallen. For if he were not looking for the resurrection of those fallen, it would have been utterly foolish to pray for the departed. But since he was looking to the reward of splendor laid up for those who repose in godliness, it was a holy and godly purpose. Thus he made atonement for the fallen, so as to set them free from their transgression. (2 Maccabees 12:40, 41–45 OSB)

Even on Pentecost Sunday, at the *Kneeling Vespers* which marks the beginning of Trinity Week, we pray not only for ourselves, but also for those who are "asleep":

> *Almighty Master, God of our fathers and Lord of mercy, Creator of mortal and immortal creatures, and of every human being who is brought forth and again dissolved, of life and death, of our sojourn here and our departure beyond, You appoint times to the living and establish the hours of death. You lead down to Hades and You lead up. You bind with weakness and release with power. You dispose all things for our use and direct what is to come for our advantage. You give life by hope of resurrection to those wounded by the sting of Death. O Master of all things, our God and Savior, the hope of all the ends of the earth and of those far off upon the sea, who on this final, great, and saving day of Pentecost revealed to us the mystery of the*

holy, consubstantial, co-eternal, undivided and uncompounded Trinity, and the coming and presence of Your Holy and Life-giving Spirit poured out in the form of tongues of fire on Your holy Apostles, making them evangelists of our true faith, revealing them as confessors and heralds of true theology; who have also been pleased on this most perfect and saving Feast to receive entreaties and prayers of atonement for those who are in Hell, granting us great hopes that repose and comfort will be sent down from You to the departed from the pains which hold them: hear us who entreat You, lowly and wretched though we are, and give rest to the souls of Your servants who have fallen asleep before us in a place of light, a place of green pasture, a place of refreshment, whence all grief, sorrow, and sighing have fled away, and establish their spirits in the courts of the righteous and count them worthy of peace and repose. For the dead will not praise You, Lord, nor do those in Hades have the freedom to offer You thanksgiving, but we the living bless You and implore You and bring before You atoning prayers and *sacrifices on behalf of their souls. (Third prayer of Kneeling Vespers, Pentecost Sunday)*

Through Christ, death is but a sleep from which we shall arise, and through baptism, even death cannot deprive us of the Church's prayers. For the Church is the Body of Christ, who is the source and wellspring of life, and there is no death in Him:

> "I am the resurrection and the life. He who believes in Me, though he may die, he shall live. And whoever lives and believes in Me shall never die." (John 11:25–26)

What precise "effect" our prayers for the departed have no one can say with any certainty. Only this we know: praying for the dead is the natural response to our belief in the survival of the soul beyond death, in our resurrection from the dead, and in the life of the age to come.

A New Heart, a New Spirit

PENTECOST SUNDAY AND TRINITY WEEK

Almighty One, renew a cherished and upright Spirit within us, to hold it eternally; the Spirit who is ever united with and ever proceeds from the Father, purging our minds of hateful matter, of burning defilements and uncleanness. (Matins of Pentecost Sunday, troparion of the sixth ode of the katavasias for Pentecost)

ON THE EVE OF PENTECOST SUNDAY, WE hear this reading from the Old Testament:

Thus says the Lord GOD: "...I will take you from among the nations, gather you out of all countries, and bring you into your own land. Then I will sprinkle clean water on you, and you shall be clean; I will cleanse you from all your filthiness and from all your idols. I will give you a new heart and put a new spirit within you; I will take the heart of stone out of your flesh and give you a heart of flesh. I will put My Spirit within you and cause you to walk in My statutes, and you will keep My judgments and do *them*. Then you shall dwell in the land that I gave to your fathers; you shall be My people, and I will be your God. I will deliver you from all your uncleannesses." (Ezek. 36:22, 24–29)

Through this reading, the themes of water and renewal are again imparted to us, reminding us once more of our renewal in the waters of baptism:

O eternal and unceasing Spring that inexpressibly gushes forth an unending river of goodness, who by Your nature ever pour forth the water of

*life, water now my thirsty soul, and set me free
from the furnace that burns with the flames of
the passions. Thus redeem me from the fearful
tribulation and dreadful torment of that fire.
(Wednesday of Trinity Week, Vespers, third
hymn of the aposticha)*

Baptism is a rebirth and regeneration. It signifies
dying to the world and living to Christ, which
means that we live for Him who is not of this
world (John 18:36). How unfortunate that so
many Christians consider such commitment to
be the vocation only of monks and clergy! In baptism, we are given the possibility of outgrowing
the "old man" (Adam) and growing into the "new"
(Christ):

*Master, Lord our God, call Your servant ... to
Your holy Illumination and count him/her
worthy of the great grace of Your holy Baptism.
Put off his/her old self and renew him/her unto
eternal life, and fill him/her with the power of
Your Holy Spirit for union with Your Christ,*

> *that he/she may no longer be a child of the body,*
> *but a child of Your kingdom. (Final prayer of*
> *the Service for Making a Catechumen)*

It is never too late to respond to this sacred calling and to renew our hearts. But let us not make the error of thinking only of "my" baptism, "my" calling, "my" salvation, as though Pentecost spoke to each individual in the Church in isolation. Pentecost is the baptism of the whole Church in the fire of the Holy Spirit and a call to unity in the Spirit of God. This is made clear in the following hymn, which describes Pentecost—when the Apostles preached, and all heard and understood in their own language (Acts 2:1–12)—as a reversal of the curse of Babel, when the nations were divided by a multitude of languages (Gen. 11:1–9):

> *When the power of the divine Spirit came down,*
> *it divinely united in one harmony the voice*
> *divided of old of those who had wickedly agreed*

together, as to believers it gave understanding
of knowledge of the Trinity, in which we have
been established. (Matins of Pentecost Sunday,
troparion of the third ode of the katavasias of
Pentecost)

Are we responding as a Church to this gift of unity in the Holy Spirit? How often we prefer division with regard to language and culture over union in the Spirit of Truth! The Holy Spirit is a spirit of unity, and in this unity we find not a flattening of human variety, but harmonious diversity: rich and poor, erudite and simple, young and old, male and female. It is the human and sinful element of the Church that often tries to turn the Church into a gathering of like-minded people with common cultural interests: a church for a particular ethnic group, a church for the young, a church for the old, a church for the super-pious.

The Holy Spirit brings in all sorts and binds them together. It is not we but the Spirit of God who makes the Church the Body of Christ and fills it with truth, wisdom, and holiness:

> The Holy Spirit bestows all things: makes proph-ecies flow, perfects priests, taught the unlettered wisdom, revealed fishermen to be theologians, welds together the whole institution of the Church. O Comforter, of one essence and equal in majesty with the Father and the Son, glory to You. (Small Vespers of Pentecost, third hymn of the stichera)

Whatever faults and errors we make as a church, let us not forget that we are yet the Church of the Holy Spirit, who is holy and divine, without sin or error. He is always with the Church, even when the Church appears to have forgotten itself, just as the disciples did: "You do not know what man-ner of spirit you are of" (Luke 9:55). But let us not be complacent, for though God is with us, we often refuse to be with Him, and so we must cry out daily for the Holy Spirit to come and dwell in us, to cleanse us, enlighten us, and guide us. For without Him, there can be no true Church, no true Christian, and no true baptism:

> *O Heavenly King, Comforter, Spirit of Truth, everywhere present and filling all things, Treasury of blessings and Giver of life, come and dwell in us, cleanse us from every stain, and save our souls, O Good One. (Vespers of Pentecost, third hymn of the aposticha)*

> *Come to us from on high, O Comforter, as You descended on the Apostles. Thus sanctify us all who proclaim You as true God. (Tuesday of Trinity Week, Matins, third hymn of the Praises for Pentecost)*

✦ 12 ✦

Vessels of the Holy Spirit

ALL SAINTS' DAY

Come, let us rejoice in spirit at the memorial of the saints; for behold, it has come bringing us gifts of grace in rich abundance. (Vespers of All Saints' Sunday, third hymn of the lity)

THE SEASON OF THE PENTECOSTARION concludes with All Saints' Day, when we remember all those who have indeed lived up to the calling of baptism; who have, by their life and death, shown themselves to be children of light and vessels of the Holy Spirit. The *Synaxarion* for the day gives us three reasons we celebrate this feast after Pentecost:

> *Our most godlike Fathers decreed that we should celebrate the present feast after the descent of the All-holy Spirit, as showing in a certain way that the coming of the All-holy Spirit acted through the Apostles like this: sanctifying and making wise human beings taken from our mortal clay and, for the completion of that fallen angelic order, restoring them and through Christ sending them to God, some by the witness of martyrdom and blood, others by their virtuous conduct and way of life; and things beyond nature are achieved.... This is one reason we celebrate the feast of All Saints....*
>
> *A second reason is that, though many people have been well-pleasing to God, they were through outstanding virtue unknown to humanity by name, or for some human reason or other, but nevertheless have great glory in God's sight. Or again, because there are many who have lived following Christ in India, Egypt, Arabia, Mesopotamia, and Phrygia,*

and in the lands beyond the Black Sea, even as far as the British Isles; in short, in both East and West, but it was not easy to honor them all properly because of their vast numbers, in the way that ecclesiastical custom has been received. And therefore, so that we may attract the help of them all, wherever on earth they were well-pleasing to God, and generally for those who would later become saints, the most godly Fathers ordained that we should celebrate the feast of All Saints, honoring the earlier and later ones, the unknown and the known—all those in whom the Holy Spirit has dwelt He has made holy.

A third reason is this. It was necessary for the saints who are celebrated individually day by day to be gathered together on one day, in order to demonstrate that, as they struggled for the one Christ and all ran the race in the same stadium of virtue, so they were all fittingly crowned as servants of one God and sustained the Church, having filled the world on high. They stir us also to accomplish the same struggle in its different and many forms, to the degree of *power that each of us has to press onwards with all eagerness. (Matins for All Saints' Sunday, Synaxarion)*

The Greek word for *saint* is *hagios,* meaning "holy one." Sainthood is therefore not the calling of a select few, but of every Christian, for God says, "Be holy, for I am holy" (1 Pet. 1:16). *Hagios* is the word St. Paul used to describe every Christian believer (e.g. Rom. 1:7; 1 Cor. 1:2; Eph. 1:1).

But how can we acquire holiness? How can we become saints? Through continuous repentance, by getting up every time we fall, by battling with our passions and forever cutting away the sin that distorts the purity and beauty of the Divine Image in which we were made. The holy Image of God is present within every one of us, but we must cut away the sin that mars and conceals it if it is to become manifest, just as a sculptor produces a work of art by the act of cutting away. This is how Michelangelo described the way he saw a work of art already completed before he even lifted a finger: "The sculpture is already complete within the marble block, before I start my work. It is already there; I just have to chisel away the superfluous material." That is a good description of the process of becoming holy.

Yet this cutting away should not lead us to think that becoming a saint means a loss of personhood. Nothing could be further from the truth! The Holy Spirit is a spirit of unity, but He is also a spirit of freedom: unity does not mean uniformity. As St. Paul writes:

> There are diversities of gifts, but the same Spirit. There are differences of ministries, but the same Lord. And there are diversities of activities, but it is the same God who works all in all. (1 Cor. 12:4–6)

Similarly, St. Cyril of Jerusalem explained how one and the same Spirit of God manifests Himself in people in various ways:

Water falls from heaven as rain, and while it is always the same in itself, it produces many different effects, one in the palm tree, another in the vine, and so on, throughout the whole of creation. It does not descend, now as one thing, now as another, but while remaining essentially the same, it adapts to the needs of every creature that receives it.

In the same way the Holy Spirit, whose nature is always the same, simple and indivisible, apportions grace to each person as He wills. Like a dry tree which puts forth shoots when watered, the soul brings forth the fruit of holiness when repentance makes it worthy of receiving the Holy Spirit. Although the Spirit never changes, the effects of His action, by the will of God and in the name of Christ, are both many and marvelous.

The Spirit makes one person a teacher of divine truth, inspires another to prophesy, gives another the power to cast out demons, enables another to interpret holy Scripture. The Spirit strengthens one person's self-control, shows another how to help the poor, teaches another to fast and lead a life of asceticism, renders another oblivious to the need of the body, trains another for martyrdom. His action is different in different people, but the Spirit Himself is always the same. *In each person,* Scripture says, *the Spirit reveals His presence in a particular way for the common good.*"[6]

As with divine gifts, so too with personalities: the Holy Spirit is not a spirit that possesses us and takes away our freedom or absorbs our personhood. The unity of the Church in the Holy Spirit does not mean a flattening of human personality. But the purity and integrity of our unique personality is distorted by sin. And so the holier we become, the more we discover our true selves.

All Saints' Day reminds us that it is possible for every one of us, however sinful we are and whatever our vocation—married or unmarried, priest or layman, scholar or simpleton—to become a

---

6   Cat. 16 De Spiritu Sancto 1, 11-12, 16: PG 33, 931-935, 939-942.

saint of the Church. At baptism, we were called to become "a holy vessel, a child of light and an heir of Your Kingdom" (third exorcism of the Baptism Service). We are all called to be saints, and through baptism we are endowed with the potential to acquire true holiness. This possibility is always at hand for every one of us. Through sincere humility, continuous repentance, and the work of the Holy Spirit within us, each of us can become a vessel of the Holy Spirit.

About the Author

ARCHIMANDRITE Vassilios Papavassiliou is a priest of the Greek Orthodox Archdiocese of Thyateira and Great Britain. He was born in London in 1977 and holds degrees in pastoral and social theology, classics, and Byzantine music. He is the author of the popular Meditations series (*Meditations for Lent, Advent,* and *Holy Week*) and *Thirty Steps to Heaven* as well as the editor of the *Ancient Faith Prayer Book.*

Also by
Vassilios Papavassiliou

Meditations for Great Lent
Reflections on the Triodion
The Lenten Triodion exhorts us, "Let us observe
a fast acceptable and pleasing to the Lord." Using
hymns from the Triodion and the Scripture
readings appointed for the season, *Meditations
for Great Lent* shows us how to make our fast
acceptable: to fast not only from food but from
sin; to fast with love and humility, as a means to
an end and not an end in itself. Keep this gem of
a book with you to inspire you for the Fast and to
dip into for encouragement as you pursue your
Lenten journey.

Meditations for Holy Week
Dying and Rising with Christ
Archimandrite Vassilios brings his liturgical and
devotional insights and warm, accessible style to
bear on the services of Holy Week, helping the
reader enter fully into this most rich and intense
period of the Christian year.

Meditations for Advent
Preparing for Christ's Birth
The author of the popular *Meditations for Great Lent* takes us through the hymnography, scripture readings, and iconography for the forty days leading up to the Nativity of Christ, showing how a full understanding of the Incarnation can enrich our spiritual lives.

Meditations for the Twelve Great Feasts
Becoming Fully Human in Christ
This volume completes the popular *Meditations* series by taking a brief look at each of the major feasts of the church year. Fr. Vassilios brings out the gems embodied in the church's hymnography to enhance our understanding and participation in these milestones of our salvation.

Thirty Steps to Heaven
The Ladder of Divine Ascent
for All Walks of Life
Many laypeople have attempted to read the great spiritual classic, *The Ladder of Divine Ascent*, but have been frustrated in attempting to apply the lessons of this monastic text to their everyday lives in the world. In *Thirty Steps to Heaven,*

Archimandrite Vassilios interprets the *Ladder* for the ordinary Christian without sacrificing any of its beauty and power. Now you too can accept the challenge offered by St. John Climacus to ascend closer to God with each passing day.

The Ancient Faith Prayer Book
Edited by Archimandrite Vassilios Papavassiliou, the *Ancient Faith Prayer Book* brings together the most ancient and popular prayers of Orthodox Christians with some additions that address issues of modern life, all rendered in elegant contemporary English and presented in a compact format for ease of use.

Ancient Faith Publishing hopes you have enjoyed and benefited from this book. The proceeds from the sales of our books only partially cover the costs of operating our nonprofit ministry—which includes both the work of **Ancient Faith Publishing** and the work of **Ancient Faith Radio.** Your financial support makes it possible to continue this ministry both in print and online. Donations are tax-deductible and can be made at www.ancientfaith.com.

To request a catalog of other publications, please call us at (800) 967-7377 or (219) 728-2216 or log onto our website: **store.ancientfaith.com**

 ANCIENT FAITH RADIO

Bringing you Orthodox Christian music, readings, prayers, teaching, and podcasts 24 hours a day since 2004 at **ancientfaith.com**